REMODEL
YOUR MIND
change your destiny

REMODEL
Your Mind
change your destiny

DARRELL MCMANUS

REMODEL YOUR MIND, CHANGE YOUR DESTINY

RevMedia Publishing
P.O. Box 5172
Kingwood, TX 77325
www.revmediapublishing.com

ISBN: 978-1-7345273-4-6
Printed in the United States of America
© 2015 Darrell McManus

DEDICATION

I dedicate this book and give all praise to the Father, the Son, and the Holy Spirit for entrusting me with this revelation. God, you are truly awesome!

I also dedicate this book to my beautiful wife, Cindy, who is my lover, friend, the mother of our children, and my faithful partner in the ministry. I love you. Without your spiritual and emotional support, this book would not have been possible. Your editing skills made my job so much easier. I love you, babe! You are the best!

In addition, I dedicate this book to my mom, Ira McManus. You have believed in me and stood by me since birth. I don't know of a finer Christian anywhere. I love you!

Finally, I dedicate this book to Pastors Ross, Beverly Cunningham, and the congregation of The Master's Gateway Church in Milano, Texas. Thank you for providing me the platform to minister on this life-changing subject. The eleven messages I delivered are the primary source for this book, and I am eternally grateful!

CONTENTS

1

UNDERSTANDING THE TRIUNE NATURE OF MAN

In this book, you will learn how to remodel your mind, which will change your destiny. In my opinion, this is one of the most-needed truths for Christians today. When I was growing up, I didn't know we were three-part beings. I thought we were two parts—soul and body. I thought that, when we came to Christ, our souls (or minds) were saved, too, and then we started walking with God.

Lack of knowledge in this area caused me to struggle with my salvation for years. I thought that when bad thoughts came into my mind, the real me was thinking them. I didn't realize that my soul (mind) hadn't been saved. But when I found this out, I was released from years of struggle. Likewise, receiving a revelation of this teaching will catapult you into the next level of your Christian walk. Get ready for the ride of your life as you enter God's remodeling room!

First Thessalonians 5:23 says, *"Now may the God of peace Himself sanctify you entirely; and may your spirit and soul and body be preserved complete, without blame at the coming of our Lord Jesus*

Christ." When God says *"entirely,"* He means all of you. This Scripture is very clear that we are three-part beings.

Genesis 2:7 tells us that the Lord God formed man of the dust of the ground. If you research the word *"dust"* in the original Hebrew, you'll find that it means "gray clay." That makes more sense, since you can form things out of clay. As I studied this verse of Scripture, I wondered, *Did God form this first man alive or dead?*

Once, I heard a preacher expounding on this verse in Genesis. He kept saying, "He made him a living soul; He made him a living soul!" And I thought, *Yes, but He formed him out of the clay.* But the man kept saying, "He made him a living soul!" Then Lord gave me wisdom: "The Lord formed man of the dust—the gray clay—of the ground, so at this point, he was *not* a living soul." What? Man was *not* a living soul? Not at this point. God could have made him alive, so why did He form him dead? He did it on purpose to illustrate a point.

Scripture goes on to say, "[God] *breathed into his nostrils the breath of life"* (Genesis 2:7). The Hebrew word for *"breath"* is *neshama,* and it's the same word translated *"spirit"* in Proverbs 20:27: *"The spirit of man is the lamp of the* LORD." So God breathed the spirit man into that dead body, and the man *became* a living soul—spirit, soul, and body—right then. Now God the Father, God the Son, and God the Holy Spirit created man in His image: spirit, soul, and body. A triune God created a triune man.

> *Now there was a man of the Pharisees, named Nicodemus, a ruler of the Jews; this man came to Jesus by night and said to Him, "Rabbi, we know that You have come from God as a teacher; for no one can do these signs that You do unless God is with him." Jesus answered and said to him, "Truly,*

truly, I say to you, unless one is born again he cannot see the kingdom of God." Nicodemus said to Him, "How can a man be born when he is old? He cannot enter a second time into his mother's womb and be born, can he?" Jesus answered, "Truly, truly, I say to you, unless one is born of the water and the Spirit he cannot enter into the kingdom of God." (John 3:1–5)

Now let me pause to explain something. We have people who are in error on this. They have clung to the belief that water baptism is what saves you, and they use this Scripture to back up their belief. Do I believe in water baptism? Yes. Why? Because Jesus said to do it. But if you aren't born again before you get water baptized, you're going down a dry sinner destined for hell and coming up a wet one! "What can wash away my sin? Nothing but the blood of Jesus"![1] Jesus said, *"Truly, truly, I say to you, unless one is born of the water **and the Spirit** he cannot enter into the kingdom of God"* (verse 5). In verse 6, He says the same thing but in a different way: *"That which is born of the flesh is flesh."* This refers to our natural, physical birth from our human mother.

Now, being born won't get you into heaven. It just means that you're "legal" on the planet. What do I mean by this? In John chapter 10, Jesus talks about the church as a sheepfold, and Himself as both its doorkeeper and shepherd. The thief (or robber) is one who enters not through the door (Jesus) but climbs in some other way. Who is the thief/robber who came up some other way, who came *"to steal and kill and destroy"* (John 10:10)? None other than Satan. Now, in order to have authority, or to be legal, on this planet, you have to have been born here. Satan was not born here and therefore doesn't have any

---

1. Robert Lowry, "Nothing but the Blood," 1876.

authority. So you can take your birth certificate and run Satan off! He doesn't have one!

> **In order to have authority, or to be legal, on this planet, you have to have been born here. Satan was not born here and therefore doesn't have any authority. So you can take your birth certificate and run Satan off! He doesn't have one!**

How did Jesus come to earth? He came through the vehicle of humanity; God set that parameter in Genesis. If He would've come any other way, then God would've lied to us, and we know from the Scriptures that God is not a liar! (See Numbers 23:19.)

In Genesis, God established some parameters, such as giving man authority on this planet. When Adam and Eve messed up, God took four thousand years to get Jesus here in a human body to fix what they had done. Four thousand years! Jesus had to find the righteous seed and establish a covenant with that righteous seed. It had to be prophesied by a human that He was coming, He had to have a "type" within the earth, and that type was established when Abraham obeyed God by offering up his son. The moment that Abraham was willing to sacrifice his Isaac, an angel stopped him and said, "God will Himself provide a sacrifice." (See Genesis 22:8.) The moment Abraham was willing to offer Isaac, then God was legally able to send Jesus to the earth through his seed.

Understanding this process helps makes sense of a lot of things. Jesus had to come through the vehicle of the flesh, through the seed of a woman, as prophesied in Genesis 3: "The seed of the woman will bruise the head of the serpent." (See Genesis 3:15.) He has ultimate authority. But the only authority Satan has is given to him by people, who have been born here. Remember, Satan is a thief and a robber; he was not born here! He can do very little unless he is given a place in a human body, your "earth-suit." You've got to take care of your earth-suit. If you lose it, you will have to leave the planet. Just as you need a space suit to live in outer space, so you need an earth-suit to live on this planet right now. The real you is in that earth-suit. The real you is a spirit being.

A New Spirit

In John 3:6, Jesus says, *"That which is born of the flesh is flesh, and that which is born of the Spirit is spirit."* In other words, being born of the flesh as a human is what gets you into this place; but the only thing that is going to get you out of this place into heaven is being born of the Holy Spirit *as a spirit.* This is what being born again is all about.

God prophesied this when He promised to give us *"one heart, and put a new spirit within* [us]" (Ezekiel 11:19). I have heard people say, "God heals your spirit when you get saved." No, that's wrong. *What God heals is the soul.* Your spirit is not healed; you get an entirely new one when you come to Christ! Scripture clearly states, *"If anyone is in Christ, he is a new crea-ture"* (2 Corinthians 5:17). This is very important! This is foundational to what we're dealing with here. Most Christians don't know this.

God said that He would take out our stony heart and dead spirit, and would put in a new heart and spirit within us. (See Ezekiel 36:26.) God the Father, in Hebrews chapter 12, says that He is the Father of spirits. He fathered your new spirit, which came straight from heaven when you were born again. And that new spirit doesn't know how to sin. When we sin, we are stepping outside of our new spirit into the flesh or the soul realm. That's why we need our souls to be saved.

When we sin, we are stepping outside of our new spirit into the flesh or the soul realm. That's why we need our souls to be saved.

You see, the Holy Spirit can't come into your spirit until you get a new spirit, because He can't come into something that is full of sin. How do we hear from God? Through our new spirit. Scripture tells us that we can pray both with the spirit and with the mind, or understanding. (See 1 Corinthians 14:15.) *The Amplified Bible* says, "I will pray…[by the Holy Spirit that is within me]." So when you are filled with the Holy Spirit, you get a new prayer language that the devil doesn't understand. It's your hotline to heaven! Look at Ezekiel 36:26–27:

> *Moreover, I will give you a new heart and put a new spirit within you; and I will remove the heart of stone from your flesh and give you a heart of flesh. I will put My Spirit within you and cause you to walk in My statutes, and you will be careful to observe My ordinances.*

The Bible speaks about the spirits of righteous men made perfect. (See Hebrews 12:23.) When you come to Christ, you are given a brand-new spirit—a perfected spirit man—straight from God, who is called *"the Father of spirits"* (Hebrews 12:9).

If you're not in Christ, then God is not your Father. He didn't father your spirit. You belong either to Him or to Satan. What do you have to do to belong to Satan? Nothing. We all have sinned and fallen short of the glory of God. (See Romans 3:23.) There's no one good—no, not one.

How does God father your spirit? How do you get a new spirit straight from the Father of spirits? You accept Jesus and make Him the Lord of your life by confessing with your mouth that He is Lord and believing in your heart that God raised Him from the dead. Then you shall be saved. There's no demon—not even Satan himself—that can stop that miracle from taking place in anybody on this planet.

Peter wrote to the Christians,

> *Blessed be the God and Father of our Lord Jesus Christ, who according to His great mercy has caused us to be born again…[and obtain] as the outcome of [our] faith the salvation of [our] souls.*   (1 Peter 1:3, 9)

In Romans 12:1, Paul encouraged believers to present their bodies as living sacrifices to God. He said, "*You…present your bodies.*" Who is "*you*"? The believer's spirit man. Paul said something else that may help you understand. He said, "*I keep under* [or "discipline"] *my body*" (1 Corinthians 9:27 KJV). Who is "*I*"? His spirit.

I have bad thoughts that come to me sometimes, but I keep them under, or discipline my mind. And they exit as quickly as they enter. Philippians 4:8 gives us six criteria by which to judge every thought that comes into our head. Every thought has to meet all six of these criteria to be able to stay in my mind.

> *Finally, brethren, whatever is **true**, whatever is **honorable**, whatever is **right**, whatever is **pure**, whatever is **lovely**,*

*whatever is of **good repute**, if there is any excellence and if anything worthy of praise, dwell on these things.*

Now look at Romans 12:2:

And do not be conformed to this world, but be transformed by the renewing of your mind, so that you may prove what the will of God is, that which is good and acceptable and perfect.

The Greek word translated *"conformed"* means "fashioned after" or "patterned after." That Greek word for *"transformed"* is *metamorphoo,* which means a transfiguration or a transformation.

A Renewed Soul

Will God do anything with your soul? Absolutely not. Look at Romans 12:2 once again. Paul said, *"Do not be conformed* [fashioned, patterned after] *to this world, but be transformed* ["metamorphoo"] *by the renewing of your mind."* Now *"mind"* is synonymous with "soul" and vice versa. So do you get a new mind or is your mind renewed? You don't get a new mind; it's got to be renewed, or a better word for it might be *restored* or *remodeled.* "Be transformed by the restoring, the remodeling, of your minds." This goes along with Psalm 23:3: *"He restores my soul."*

Have you ever restored a piece of furniture? If you have, you know you don't just come in with new paint and stick it on! You have to take off all the old stuff first, and it takes a lot of work. I've asked carpenters if they would rather start a new construction or remodel an old one? All of them said they'd rather do a new construction. Why? Fresh lumber—they don't have to take out anything. They have all new materials.

Likewise, when you come to Christ, your *spirit* is like a new construction. You receive a new spirit, and if you have been filled with the Holy Spirit, you've got a head start. However, your *soul* is a remodeling project. You can't put the Word into an old soul without first taking out what's there, so you have room to receive it.

And so, there are people with unrenewed minds going along for months and months trying to appropriate the Word. Yes, they're getting the Word into their *spirit*, but there's not much happening in the *soul*.

Pay attention here: You're not going to find out the will of God for your life just because you have been born again and have received a new spirit. You're not going to be able to find out the will of God for your life until your soul is restored. *"But be transformed by the renewing [remodeling] of your mind, so that you may prove what the will of God is, that which is good and acceptable and perfect."* Who's going to prove what the will of God is? You! But not until your mind has been remodeled.

You're not going to find out the will of God for your life just because you have been born again and have received a new spirit. You're not going to be able to find out the will of God for your life until your soul is restored.

What is this remodeling process? Isaiah 26:3 (KJV) says, *"Thou wilt keep him in perfect peace, whose mind is stayed on thee."* *"Stayed"* comes from the Hebrew word *yatsar*, which means "a form; figuratively, conception (i.e. purpose)—frame, thing framed, imagination, mind, work"[2] The remodeling process of the mind is when the mind is "framed" with God's building material. God says that we're not to be conformed to this world but to be transformed by the remodeling of our minds. Remodel means to tear out the old material, so that we can put new material in. You see, sometimes during construction, people find old, moldy wood behind Sheetrock walls. Similarly, a lot of Christians come to church and praise God, but inside they are full of "old wood." God will only keep him in perfect peace whose mind is framed with the Word of God, whose mind is new, fresh, and straight.

The new birth of your spirit is the beginning of your faith; the saving of your soul is the goal, or the end, of your faith; and getting your new body is the completion of your faith. You'll be whole on that day! You may wonder, *What will I do when the rotten lumber is pulled out of me?* Well, that thought itself is like rotten lumber. Remove it and toss it away, and replace it immediately with a new piece of lumber—a new, righteous thought, according to the Word. Replace it with God's lumber, restoring the soul man, having the mind of Christ, so that you can prove what is the good and acceptable and perfect will of God.

---

2. *yatsar, Strong's Exhaustive Concordance*, http://biblehub.com/hebrew/3336.htm.

2

TAKING A CLOSER LOOK AT BODY, SOUL, AND SPIRIT

As we saw in the last chapter, many Christians, after being born again, don't remodel their souls; so they have a very difficult time getting into the Word. They say, "I'm trying to study the Word, but it's hard; I just don't get it!" The reason they don't "get it" is because the remodeling process never started in their souls. As I said, the soul includes your mind; so to remodel your soul, you must deal with your mind: your thoughts and your feelings.

The end, or goal, of our faith is the salvation of our souls. (See 1 Peter 1:9.) So what's the beginning of our faith? The new birth of our spirits.

The Amplified Bible says, "The strong spirit of a man sustains him in bodily pain or trouble, but a weak **and** broken spirit who can raise up **or** bear?" (Proverbs 18:14). So we find that the spirit man can sustain a person if it's strong—and you need it strong. The only kind of food that will grow your spirit is the Word of God, and the same food that will grow your spirit will save your soul. Now, even though the spirit of man will sustain you if there's an illness attacking your body, it will not make you well. Health is connected to what's going on in your soul.

If you have a new spirit and a remodeled mind, the two will team up on your body. And when that happens, sickness will grow legs and walk away from you. The mind is where the images are formed. *"For as* [a man] *thinketh in his heart, so is he"* (Proverbs 23:7 KJV). So if you focus on the things above and concentrate each day on speaking the Word over your body, your finances, your home, and your relationships, your soul will come into alignment with your new spirit. Scripture says, *"Beloved, I pray that in all respects you may prosper and be in good health, just as your soul prospers"* (3 John 2)Furthermore, in Proverbs 4:20–21, we find God's prescription for health: God said,

1. *"Give attention to my words,"* or *"Put My words first."*

2. *"Incline your ear to my sayings."*"*Do not let them depart from your sight."* *"Keep them in the midst of your heart."*

What are you looking at? What are you hearing? What's coming through your ear and eye gates? You can have God's Word all over your house, but unless you get it down into your spirit, it won't do you any good. Does medicine do you any good if it sits on the shelf? Get the medicine of the Word into your spirit!

> ## You can have God's Word all over your house, but unless you get it down into your spirit, it won't do you any good.

A lot of Christians don't realize that they are three-part beings. But 1 Thessalonians 5:23 tells us that we are spirit, soul, and body. To make this even clearer, we are a spirit, we have a soul, and we live in a body. Now it's very important to know that the Lord desires that all three parts of us are preserved until He comes. Let me give you three Greek words synonymous with spirit, soul, and body.

1. *Pneuma* is translated *"spirit"* in the Scriptures. It's the same Greek word whether it's referring to the Holy Spirit or your human spirit. For this reason, every time you see the word "spirit" in the New Testament, you have to look at the context to see whether it's referring to the Holy Spirit or to the human spirit. Of course, in John 3:6, when Jesus was talking to Nicodemus, He said, *"That which is born of the Spirit is spirit."* Here, both instances are "pneuma," but the first refers to *the* Spirit, the Holy Spirit, and the second refers to the human spirit. And so, your "pneuma," or spirit man, was born of the Holy Spirit.

2. *Psuche* is translated *"soul"* in the Scriptures, which includes the mind, the will, and the emotions. The mind has at least two parts: thoughts and feelings.

3. *Soma* is translated *"body"* in the Scriptures, so every time you see *"body"* in the New Testament, it comes from the word *soma*. Furthermore, you'll see the word *"flesh"* in Scriptures, which comes from the Greek word *sarx*,[3] as in 2 Corinthians 10:3–5 (KJV), which says,

Though we walk in the flesh, we do not war after the flesh: (for the weapons of our warfare are not carnal [flesh-ruled], but mighty through God to the pulling down of strong holds;) casting down imaginations, and every high thing that exalteth itself against the knowledge of God, and bringing into captivity every thought to the obedience of Christ.

---

3. *sarx*, http://biblehub.com/greek/4561.htm.

Now the things of God should have a stronghold in us. Those are not the things we should be pulling down. The strongholds mentioned in 2 Corinthians 10:3–5, however, are of a fleshly nature, and so we must learn to cast down imaginations and bring into captivity every thought to the obedience of Christ.

Now let me ask you a question. What's the context there? Who is going to be *"bringing into captivity every thought"*? According to the Scriptures, we are! Like the saying goes, "If it's going to be, it's up to me!" When I say "me," who am I referring to? My spirit man!

Remember: You are a spirit, you have a soul, and you live in a body. Paul said, *"I keep under my body"* (1 Corinthians 9:27 KJV), which tells us that our bodies aren't us. So many times, we go through life and something unsettling happens. That's the enemy trying to muddy the water. Perhaps an illness comes or depression tries to hit us, and the world says, "That's you: You're messed up!" But let's separate fact from fiction, as they say. Your body and your soul—your mind, will, emotions, thoughts, feelings, and affections—are not you.

Scripture says that the body without the spirit is dead (the "soma" without the "pnuema"). (See James 2:26.) That's pretty clear, isn't it? Sometimes, you have to study Scripture to fully grasp all this. That's why Paul told Timothy, *"Study to shew thyself approved unto God, a workman who needeth not to be ashamed, rightly dividing the word of truth"* (2 Timothy 2:15 KJV). In other words, without studying, we can wrongly divide the Word.

So, if your soma (your body) is sick, that doesn't mean that you are sick, and there are keys to getting the soma well.

We know that the beginning of our faith is the new birth of our spirits (see Ezekiel 36:26) and that the end (or goal) of our faith is the salvation of our souls (see 1 Peter 1:9). Remember in John 3, where Jesus told Nicodemus, *"That which is born of the Spirit is spirit"* (John 3:6)? Another Scripture says, *"Therefore if any man* [the spirit man] *be in Christ, he is a new creature: old things are passed away; behold, all things are become new"* (2 Corinthians 5:17 KJV). This process did not happen in your soul or in your body—*it happened in your spirit.* Your soul—your mind, your will, and your emotions—is connected to your physical prospering, or the health of your body, and yet a lot of Christians neglect the soul realm. Once a person comes to Christ, he still needs the saving of his soul; this should be his number one goal. Outside of being water baptized, getting filled with the Spirit, and getting into a good Bible-believing church, *he needs a saved soul!*

Maintaining the soul realm is where marriages fall apart. I recently found out about another Christian marriage that had fallen apart, a couple who had been in our ministry years ago. They both had the call of God on their lives and were moving in the direction of the Lord, and I guarantee you that it all began to unravel in the soul realm. Thoughts and feelings all lie in the soul realm, and many Christians live and die without any sancification ever really taking place in their souls. They're in heaven, but they caused a big, jumbled-up mess while they were down here!

Thoughts and feelings all lie in the soul realm, and many Christians live and die without any sancification ever really taking place in their souls. They're in heaven, but they caused a big, jumbled-up mess while they were down here!

Let's zero in on the mind for a few moments: We're to be *transformed* by the renewing of our minds. Remember, *transform* comes from the Greek word *metamorphoo*, which means "change." It's like the Hulk character. One minute there's Bruce Banner—a pretty normal-looking guy—and then something happens, and he changes into this huge green being. Now that's a bad metamorphosis. The problem is, we have Christians with born-again—and even Spirit-filled—spirits, and yet their souls aren't saved. During the week, the green Hulk comes out growling and snarling in their souls. But remember, their souls aren't them. They have souls, and they have to do something with them.

Paul says we are to be transformed by the renewing (or remodeling) of our minds. Now, remember, this process is just like home renovation , in which you've got to tear out the old before you can put in the new. Isaiah 26:3 (kjv) says, "*Thou wilt keep him in perfect peace, whose mind is stayed* [framed] *on thee.*" Every thought that comes into your mind is like a stud: It's either a bad stud or a good stud. If it's a bad stud, just chuck it out! You're constructing something, you're building a structure in your mind, so use only good studs! Remember, the soul is also connected to healing in your body. Sickness and disease are sometimes the results of building the wrong structures in your mind. If they become strongholds, then the anointing needs to destroy that thing. You must keep rejecting that bad lumber— thoughts of sickness, disease, and so forth.

The Bible instructs us to "*gird up the loins of your mind*" (1 Peter 1:13 kjv). Who's going to gird it up? We are. Here's another Scripture that shows that our minds are not us. The Greek word for "*loins*" is *osphus*, which means "the lower region of the back," "[the] lumbar region...as opposed to shoulders and thighs," "the reproduction organs."[4] In other words, what you're producing is connected to what you're girding up in the loins of your mind.

If not stopped, every attack will manifest in three stages:

1. Thoughts: Thoughts are either good studs or bad studs. When a thought comes, you must choose whether or not you're going to use it to frame and construct or toss it out. You will have to chuck most thoughts.

2. Imagination: This is where the framing process takes place. Be careful what kind of studs (thoughts) you allow into your mind, because your imagination will take them and run with them!

3. Stronghold: If you don't reject those wrong thoughts, if you let them take hold in your mind and frame themselves there, then you will be creating a structure, a stronghold, that may cause sickness, depression, and so forth. It may cause you to isolate yourself from the church you're supposed to be in, or the ministry you're supposed to be a part of.

Peter exhorts us to "be sober" (see 1 Peter 5:8), but you can't be sober unless you gird up the loins of your mind, or as the *New American Standard Bible* translates, *"Prepare your minds for action."* We are also instructed, *"Be ye holy, for I am holy"* (1 Peter 1:16 KJV). What you are doing or not doing with your mind determines whether or not you are holy. It has nothing to do with your spirit—your spirit was instantly holy when you were born again.

Now it came about when Rachel had borne Joseph, that Jacob said to Laban, "Send me away, that I may go to my

---

4. *osphus*, http://www.sermonindex.net/modules/articles/index. php?view=article&aid=34384.

own place and to my own country. Give me my wives and my children for whom I have served you, and let me depart; for you yourself know my service which I have rendered you." But Laban said to him, "If now it pleases you, stay with me; I have divined that the Lord has blessed me on your account." He continued, "Name me your wages, and I will give it." But he said to him, "You yourself know how I have served you and how your cattle have fared with me. For you had little before I came and it has increased to a multitude, and the Lord has blessed you wherever I turned. But now, when shall I provide for my own household also?" So he said, "What shall I give you?" And Jacob said, "You shall not give me anything. If you will do this one thing for me, I will again pasture and keep your flock: let me pass through your entire flock today, removing from there every speckled and spotted sheep and every black one among the lambs and the spotted and speckled among the goats; and such shall be my wages. So my honesty will answer for me later, when you come concerning my wages. Every one that is not speckled and spotted among the goats and black among the lambs, if found with me, will be considered stolen." Laban said, "Good, let it be according to your word." So he removed on that day the striped and spotted male goats and all the speckled and spotted female goats, every one with white in it, and all the black ones among the sheep, and gave them into the care of his sons. And he put a distance of three days' journey between himself and Jacob, and Jacob fed the rest of Laban's flocks. (Genesis 30:25–36)

Jacob told Laban that he could remove all the spotted and speckled sheep and goats and all the black lambs from his herd, and that whatever spotted and speckled sheep the remainder solid-colored sheep and goats bore would be his. Jacob had a plan, and he believed God for a miracle. You see, Jacob knew that the loins—the reproductive organs—were in the mind, and that they were also in the minds of those sheep and goats.

So after agreeing to the deal, Laban removed the speckled and spotted male goats and all the speckled and spotted female goats, plus the ones with white on them and all the black lambs— and he gave them to his sons to take care of. He removed everything that would become any wages for Jacob; he removed all the genetics for what Jacob needed.

Not only did he remove all the spotted and speckled sheep and goats, but Laban took the flocks and put a three days' journey between them and Jacob.

So Jacob fed the remainder of Laban's flocks—solid colored goats and sheep. Jacob took poles of poplar and almond and plain trees and peeled strips of bark, making white stripes in them. Basically, he made pictures of spots and speckles for the cattle to look at. Remember: Everything starts with a thought. He set those rods in front of the flocks by the watering troughs. So every time the cattle came to drink water, they saw spots and speckles.

What happened next? When the cattle were in heat and came to drink, they mated by the water troughs. They didn't know they were solid-colored cattle! They had girded up the loins of their minds and their reproductive organs as they'd looked at all those spots and speckles! Now these were sheep and goats with no genetics for spots or speckles! Jacob proposed a deal that made it so difficult for him to prosper; in fact, it took a miracle by the hand of God to make him prosper. So here's something for you to ponder today: What have *you* been looking at? What has your mind been focused on? Because I can tell you, that's the structure that's within you right now. And it will affect your body. It will affect every part of your life.

What have *you* been looking at? What has your mind been focused on?... That's the structure that's within you right now. And it will affect your body. It will affect every part of your life.

It's all about what you're putting in your mind! You may have a chronic illness or chronic depression, perhaps it has plagued you for years, but I want to tell you, when the thought structure starts to change in the reproductive organs of your mind, it will affect your entire being. God can transform your thought life.

"*Wherefore gird up the loins of your mind*" (1 Peter 1:13 KJV). Who is this addressed to? Obviously the mind is not *you*, so who is Peter addressing? He's addressing the real you, *the spirit man*. It is the job of the spirit man to "*gird up the loins of the mind.*" It's your job to take authority over your mind.

We learned earlier that the Greek word for "loins" is *osphus*, so we are commanded to gird up the *osphus*, or reproductive organs, of our minds. What you keep looking at, what you keep in front of your mind, is going to reproduce, good or bad, just like Jacob's cattle. So what have you been thinking about? What have you been keeping in the front of your mind, in front of your soul realm—your mind, your will, and your emotions? That's what is going to impact your life.

Do you know that health is not related to how your spirit's doing, but to how your soul is doing? Third John 2 says, "*Beloved, I pray that in all respects you may prosper and be in good health, just as your soul prospers."* There are things I won't look at; things I refuse to keep in the front of Darrell McManus' mind. When I see a flu commercial during flu season, I immediately mute it; and you'll hear me speak out to the contrary: "Not here—no flu will enter this house!" The Bible tells us that death and life are in the power of the tongue, and that we will reap the fruit of it. (See Proverbs 18:21.) What does that mean? It means that those who speak life-filled words will have life and those who speak death-filled words will have death.

So, back to those spotted and speckled sheep and goats. What happened? The solid-colored sheep and goats started producing offspring that weren't even in their genetics. They started reproducing spotted and speckled cattle! Why? Because Jacob kept the "speckled" image in front of their eyes and minds. The Bible says, *"For as* [a man] *thinketh in his heart, so is he"* (Proverbs 23:7 KJV).

3

THE
PHILIPPIANS 4:8 TEST

*"Finally, brethren, whatever is true, whatever is honorable,
whatever is right, whatever is pure, whatever is lovely,
whatever is of good repute, if there is any excellence and if
anything worthy of praise, dwell on these things."*
—Philippians 4:8

Recently, I looked at the framework of boards on the outside
of a house and compared it to the framing in my own mind. Every
thought that comes into my mind is either like an old, rotten stud
or a clean, new one. Everyday, I throw all the bad studs out and
look for good ones I can frame my mind with. Every one of you is
framing, or constructing, something in your mind, good or bad.
That's why we read in 2 Corinthians 10:3–5 (KJV),

> *For though we walk in the flesh, we do not war after the
> flesh: (for the weapons of our warfare are not carnal, but
> mighty through God to the pulling down of strong holds;)
> casting down imaginations...and bringing into captivity
> every thought to the obedience of Christ.*

Everything in life starts with a thought, and this is where strongholds develop. If you dwell on thoughts long enough, they will become imaginations. Beware of imagination: It's the biggest "nation" in the world, because it has no end! And if you stay in that nation long enough, it will become a stronghold, and a stronghold is just like the enemy's hand upon your head.

Therefore, I am going to give you six criteria by which to judge every thought that comes into your head. Your thoughts will have to pass these six tests in order to qualify as good lumber from God. Now, what if you already have a structure built of rotten lumber in your head? Well, that is where the anointing is needed, because it can pull all that bad lumber out in a moment. I want you to envision every thought that comes into your mind as a stud, which is used in constructing something in your head. How many of you want a whole bunch of rotten lumber in your heads? I doubt any of you, so be careful what you dwell on. One way to do this is to try every thought by the Philippians 4:8 Test:

The Philippians 4:8 Test

> *Finally, brethren, whatever is true, whatever is honorable, whatever is right, whatever is pure, whatever is lovely, whatever is of good repute, if there is any excellence and if anything worthy of praise, dwell on these things.*

1. *"Whatever is true."* The Greek word translated *"true"* is *aléthés*, which means "unconcealed, true,…worthy of credit."[5] A lot of times, people carry thoughts of gossip. Do these thoughts meet the criteria of *aléthés*? Most thoughts that come to you in a day's time are going to be rotten lumber! So you have a choice whether to entertain them or not. You're

---

5. *aléthés, Strong's Concordance,* http://biblehub.com/greek/227.htm.

going to have to make some decisions. If somebody came to your house with a truck full of garbage, knocked on your door, and said, "We've got garbage to leave at this address," how many of you would say, "Well, come on in!" Of course, you wouldn't! If it's not *aléthés*—if it's not unconcealed, true, or worthy of credit—then don't allow it in! This is checkpoint No. 1.

2. *"Whatever is honorable."* "Honorable" comes from the Greek word *semnós*, which means "venerable, honorable, and dignified."[6] Now a thought might pass the first test (*aléthés*)—in other words, it might be unconcealed, true, and worthy of credit—but it might not pass the second test; it might not be "venerable, honorable, and dignified." I challenge you to run every thought that comes to you in a day's time by the Philippians 4:8 Test. In order for it to qualify as a good stud to build with in your mind, it's got to pass all six of these checkpoints. You can see why we have so many problems in the body of Christ. I'm not talking about sinners here; I'm talking about people who have Jesus but still have garbage in their heads. Remember, health is related to how our souls are doing!*"Whatever is right."* The King James Version says it this way: *"Whatsoever things are just."* The original word for *"right"* is *dikaios*, which means "innocent, holy...just...right(-eous)."[7] You mean something can be true and worthy of credit but not as it should be? Yes, and if it doesn't pass this part of the Philippians 4:8 Test, then you shouldn't keep it in your mind. The thought has to be "innocent, holy...just...right(-eous)," or, as I woud say, evenhanded justice. If a thought lacks evenhanded justice,

---

6. *semnós, Strong's Concordance,* http://biblehub.com/greek/4586.htm.
7. *dikaios, Strong's Exhaustive Concordance,* http://biblehub.com/greek/1342.htm.

then it doesn't qualify to be entertained. No ifs, ands, or buts about it! It doesn't qualify. You talk about an overhaul of the body of Christ overnight: If everybody who claims to be a Christian would take the Philippians 4:8 Test for twenty-four hours, holding his or her mind to the principles of this Scripture, we would see the most radical change in the body of Christ since its inception. The last meaning of *dikaios* is "impartial."[8] If any judgment or thought shows partiality, don't think on it; don't allow it room in your mind.

3. *"Whatever is pure."* The Greek word for *"pure"* is *hagnos*, and it means "innocent, modest, perfect, chaste, clean."[9] In other words, think only on clean thoughts. Some of you may say, "Well, the enemy just bombards my mind!" Let me tell you, you can interrupt your own thoughts. Don't believe me? Try counting from one to one hundred and, in the process, say out loud your whole given name. What will happen? You will interrupt your thoughts! James says that the tongue is like a rudder. (See James 3:4–5.) That's why the tongue is the only member that shows evidence of the filling of the Holy Spirit, because it can overrides everything else in your life. So, if you can get the Word of God in your mind and quote Scriptures easily and effortlessly, you will stop negative thoughts! Most days, it takes me about thirty minutes to focus my mind on the Word of God and speak it aloud. I can tell you that most days, my mind does not want to do it; most days, my mind wants to focus on something unholy. I'm being honest here!

---

8. *dikaios, Strong's Concordance,* http://biblehub.com/greek/1342.htm.
9. *hagnos, Strong's Exhaustive Concordance,* http://biblehub.com/greek/53.htm.

If you can get the Word of God in your mind and quote Scriptures easily and effortlessly, you will stop negative thoughts!

4. *"Whatever is lovely."* The Greek word for *"lovely"* is *prosphilés*, which causes "pleasure or delight…lovely, amiable."[10] Psalm 16:11 (KJV) says, *"Thou wilt shew me the path of life: in thy presence is fulness of joy; at thy right hand there are pleasures for evermore."* So, if it doesn't cause pleasure or delight, if it's not lovely, then don't keep that stud in your mind. Don't build with that. This may require changing some of what you're listening to. You may have to change what source you consult for information. And those will be great changes. Remember, God has made *you* the custodian of your mind.

5. *"Whatever is of good repute."* The King James Version says, *"Of good report."* The Greek word here is *euphémos*, which means "sounding well, uttering words of good omen… things spoken in a kindly spirit, with good-will to others"[11] and "praiseworthy."[12] There are a lot of things in life that can be true and real but don't deserve praise. The moment you let them into your mind, you are saying, in effect, "This deserves my praise." Believe me, I have to live this, too. It's easy to teach on it, but living it is much harder! The doer is blessed. Didn't James say, "Be a doer, not a forgetful hearer"? (See James 1:22.) A hearer only of the Word is like a man who looks in a mirror, sees who he is, but then walks away

---

10. *prosphilés, Bauer-Danker Greek Lexicon of the New Testament.*
11. *euphémos, Thayer's Greek Lexicon,* http://biblehub.com/greek/2163.htm.
12. *euphémos, Strong's Exhaustive Concordance,* http://biblehub.com/greek/2163.htm.

and forgets what he looks like. By the time he comes home from work, he has so many rotten studs in his head, he's ready to kick down the walls! Transformation takes place, all right, but the man is like Bruce Banner in *The Incredible Hulk!* The monster comes out! Be like Superman, who goes into the phone booth of God's Word and comes out with the good stuff! These are the six criteria for framing your mind. If your thoughts pass all six Philippians 4:8 checkpoints, then dwell on those thoughts. Think on anything that is true, honorable, right, pure, lovely, of good repute; furthermore, *"if there is any excellence* [moral goodness, moral excellence, or good conduct] *and if anything worthy of praise* [commendation, recognition, expressing admiration], *dwell on these things."*

In closing, the Greek word for *"dwell"* in this Scripture is *logizomai*, which means "to determine by a mathematical process."[13] So, *"dwell"* means to use math, and a mathematical process reckons, calculates, and takes inventory. How do *you* take inventory? When a thought comes, ask yourself, Is it true? Yes! Is it honest? Yes! Is it just? Yes! Is it pure? Yes! Is it lovely? Yes! Is it of a good report? Yes! Then build with it!

---

13. *logizomai, Bauer-Danker Greek Lexicon of the New Testament.*

4

REINING IN THE SOUL MAN

You can't live on this planet without framing something in your mind. So, why not frame according to God's plan? *"As [a man] thinketh in his heart, so is he"* (Proverbs 23:7 KJV). First Peter 1:6, 9 (NKJV) says, *"The end [or goal] of your faith [is] the salvation of your souls."* The birth of my new spirit is the beginning of my faith. God is a Spirit, and I am a spirit. We know that *"those who worship Him must worship in spirit and truth"* (John 4:24). You can't worship God from the soul realm; but many times, you will have to start off praising Him through the soul realm. We'll get into that a bit later.

You don't have to command your spirit, but you do have to command your soul. In the garden of Gethsemane, Jesus's disciples couldn't stay awake to pray with Him for even one hour, which was all He was asking for. Jesus looked at them and said, *"You men could not keep watch with Me for one hour?"* (Matthew 26:40). It's amazing how many Christians can't pray for even one hour. Then look at what Jesus said: *"The spirit is willing, but the flesh is weak"* (verse 40). Our flesh man is weak. And so, we have another demonstration of the three-part being—body, soul, and spirit. Only the saved soul can win over the flesh in your life. It is a democracy inside you: The majority vote wins every day of your life. An unsaved soul will always side with the flesh. The spirit man will be dragged along, kicking and screaming, "No, I want to pray, I want to pray!" Jesus said that your spirit is willing, but your flesh is weak. It's imperative that, as Christians, you and I get on with the business of getting our soul man saved.

Now, there are times when you will have to make drastic cuts of thoughts in your soul. When I say "you" have to take drastic measures, I mean the *real* you, the spirit man. You have to realize that all those rotten thoughts that come to you are not *you*. It's your job to chuck those studs out of your head and start framing with good lumber. Remember the Philippians 4:8 Test: Get a hold of those six principles for godly thinking and use them to sift your thoughts.

Sometimes you have to shock your soul into obedience. And one way to do that is to humble the soul man.

But as for me, when they were sick, my clothing was sackcloth; I humbled my soul with fasting.   (Psalm 35:13)

There are some things you cannot accomplish without prayer and fasting. What does it mean to humble the soul man? It means shutting down the emotions; shutting down the mind and the will. If I can humble my soul man, then I can start hearing from the Spirit. There are times when you just have to say, "Okay, you're going to do without (fill in the blank)." Maybe it's the newspaper or the TV. Everybody has something that tries to latch on to him/her as a habit. I challenge you, try to say no to your soul man for a day.

I remember a minister who said he liked to drink ice tea, so he would tell his soul man, "No, you're not going to have it this time" just to prove that it didn't have control over him.

The Bible says that the *love* of money is the root of all evil. (See 1 Timothy 6:10.) This gets so misquoted! Many people say that money is the root of all evil. The love of money means that someone is controlled by money; it has them. If you don't love money, you have control over it. If you have money, then God can say, "Go give to such-and-such," and you'll do it. That's proof that you have money. If money has you, on the other hand, then you will be like the rich young ruler, who walked away from Christ with all his possessions. (See Matthew 19:21–22.) Jesus didn't care that he had money; He just wanted to see if money had him.

> Many people say that money is the root of all evil. The love of money means that someone is controlled by money; it has them. If you don't love money, you have control over it.

The mouth is the locator. It always locates where we're at. Now, the natural man (the sinner) has no control over his mouth—or very little, at best. But Christians should have total control if they are operating out of the Spirit. If Christians operate out of the flesh, they will act and sound just like the natural man. According to Scripture, the spiritual man has insight into people's lives, but no one has insight into him. (See 1 Corinthians 2:15.) Who is a spiritual man? Someone who is saved, born again, full of the Word, and full of the Holy Spirit.

Then there's the carnal man: You cannot be a carnal man unless you're a Christian. So the sinner can't be a carnal man?

No, because the Bible says that the sinner is a "natural" man. It also says that the natural man can't receive the things of God. (See 1 Corinithans 2:14 KJV.) The natural man or woman must be born again. If you study the first three chapters of 1 Corinthians, you will read about these three types of men. Paul, when discussing the carnal man, was talking to a Spirit-filled, tongues-speaking church, and he told them, "You're carnal!" (see 1 Corinthians 3:1) or "flesh-ruled." They were saved, and they still loved Jesus. The problem was that people couldn't tell that by the way they were living. A carnal person hasn't denied Jesus; he hasn't completely turned his back on the Lord, either. His soul isn't saved, that's all. We're finding out that the saving of our souls is the end of our faith. And we can obtain it. Here's a scenario for you. Suppose you're in a long line at a grocery store and people are getting frustrated because they've got to be other places. There are plenty of natural people there, fuming and fussing—maybe even throwing some items and cussing—but there are very few spiritual people whose souls have been saved and are ruled by the Spirit in the mix. Then there are the carnal Christians, who are "mirror men," acting like the rest of the group when they should be behaving according to the dictates of the Spirit of God.

Again, there's very little difference between the life of a natural person and the life of a carnal person. The natural person is *not* saved, while the carnal Christian is: he has embraced Jesus and has a new spirit, but his life still doesn't line up with the Word of God; his spirit is saved, but his soul is not. That's the kind of person who has a fish bumper sticker on his car but, when he gets cutoff on the freeway, loses his cool. The fish turns into a shark.

The natural person is *not* saved, while the carnal Christian is: he has embraced Jesus and has a new spirit, but his life still doesn't line up with the Word of God; his spirit is saved, but his soul is not.

James said, "*Wherefore lay apart all filthiness and superfluity of naughtiness, and receive with meekness the engrafted word, which is able to save your souls*" (James 1:21 KJV). Their souls weren't saved, so James had to tell them what to do to be saved. Let's look at this Scripture for a few moments—this is powerful stuff here!

This Scripture has changed my life—it changes it every day—and it'll change your life and your walk, too, if you let it. Here are some of the original Greek words in James 1:21:

1. "*Lay apart*" comes from the Greek word *apotithémi*, which means to "cast off, lay aside, put away."[14]

2. "*Filthiness*" comes from the Greek word *rhuparia*, which means "pollution, defilement."[15] Filthiness can lead to obscenity and adultery, and adultery destroys not only a marriage but also a soul. Look at Proverbs 6:32 (NKJV): "*Whoever commits adultery with a woman lacks understanding; he who does so destroys his own soul.*" If we obey James 1:21, we will never have a problem with that.

3. "*Superfluity*" comes from the Greek word *perisseia*, which means "abundance, surplus."[16]

---

14. *apotithémi*, *Strong's Exhaustive Concordance*, http://biblehub.com/greek/659.htm.

15. *rhuparia*, *Strong's Concordance*, http://biblehub.com/greek/4507.htm.

16. *perisseia*, *Strong's Exhaustive Concordance*, http://biblehub.com/greek/4050.htm.

4. *"Naughtiness"* comes from the Greek word *kakia*, which means "malice, ill-will, desire to injure [another person]."[17] We should never desire to injure another human being.

5. *"Receive"* is from the Greek word *dechomai*, which means to "take, receive, accept, welcome."[18] It means to receive as a self-prompted action, to make room for something, to welcome or receive with my mind. In other words, once I throw filthiness and naughtiness out of my life, then I (the real me) will make room for the engrafted Word.

6. *"Meekness"* comes from the Greek word *prautés*, which means "mildness, gentleness."[19] It is also sometimes translated *"humility"* (KJV).

7. *"Engrafted"* comes from the Greek word *emphutos*, which means "inborn [in heart]…rooted, implanted."[20] The Word cannot take root in your heart until you throw off filthiness and naughtiness. And if the Word can't take root, then it can't grow. That's why a Christian can sit under gospel preaching week after week after week but never see a change. All this has to be done before your soul can receive the Word and be saved.

How does one receive the Word? By reading it and by studying it. We *all* need to do this! We study "to show ourselves approved, workmen who need not be ashamed." (See 2 Timothy 2:15.) You can have hands laid on you till there's no more hair on your head—or until the Lord puts some on—to save your soul, but it won't work. The Word alone is what keeps you. I don't care if you jump, leap, dance, or run as long as, when your feet hit the floor, you have enough Word in you to walk straight. The rooted

17. *kakia*, *Thayer's Greek Lexicon*, http://biblehub.com/greek/2549.htm.
18. *dechomai*, *Strong's Concordance*, http://biblehub.com/greek/1209.htm.
19. *prautés*, *Strong's Concordance*, http://biblehub.com/greek/4240.htm.
20. *emphutos*, *Strong's Concordance*, http://biblehub.com/greek/1721.htm.

Word has the power to save your soul. It's not the Word you've been under but the Word that's taken root in you.

The rooted Word has the power to save your soul. It's not the Word you've been under but the Word that's taken root in you.

We have to learn the power of focusing our minds. We're not talking about Transcendental Meditation here. Those who promote Transcendental Meditation get their ideas from the devil, who hasn't created anything original. Look at what he promotes, and there will not be anything original about it. God established meditation when He instructed Joshua to meditate on the Word day and night. (See Joshua 1:8.)

> *So if you were raised along with the Messiah, then seek the things above, where the Messiah is **sitting at the right hand of God**. Focus your minds on the things above, not on things here on earth.*   (Colossians 3:1–2 CJB)

Whose job is that? The *real* you; it's *your* job to focus your mind.

How often are we to be setting our minds on things above? Constantly. How often are we to focus our minds on things above? Constantly.

We have to focus our minds on things above. It's not easy, but it's always worth it!

5

THE THREE TYPES OF MAN AND HOW THEY AFFECT THE SPIRIT

Now may the God of peace Himself sanctify you entirely; and may your spirit and soul and body be preserved complete, without blame at the coming of our Lord Jesus Christ.
—1 Thessalonians 5:23

Now, when Scripture says *"entirely,"* or "wholly," it means all. In this instance, *"entirely"* means that human beings consists of spirit, soul, and body. This is what every human is made of, right here. You see, it is God's will that you are completely saved when He comes back. However, a lot of Christians are only born again. God, as we have seen from Scripture, is called *"the Father of spirits"*:

> *But if you are without discipline, of which all have become partakers, then you are illegitimate children and not sons. Furthermore, we had earthly fathers to discipline us, and we respected them; shall we not much rather be subject to the Father of spirits, and live?* (Hebrews 12:8–9)

Everyone who doesn't know Jesus has a dead spirit. They are the "dead walking." Most people on this earth wake up each morning and walk around dead. The dead walking are not on death row; they just don't have a new spirit. "Dead walking" means that your body's alive, but your spirit (the real you) is dead.

So, what happens when we're born again? God the Father breathes a new spirit into our body. Once that happens, we are to be subject to Him as He disciplines us; because He disciplines us *"that we may share His holiness"* (Hebrews 12:10). Holiness is our walk! If we subject ourself, our spirit, to the Father of spirits, then we will be holy as He is holy. Scripture says, *"Be ye holy"* (1 Peter 1:16 KJV); notice it doesn't say, "Get holy." If we're subject to the Father of your spirit, we will *be* holy! Hebrews 12:11 tells us that all discipline for the moment seems sorrowful; so why does the Father of spirits discipline you and me? To train us! *"Afterwards it yields the peaceful fruit of righteousness"* (Hebrews 12:11).

There is the gift of righteousness, and there is the fruit of righteousness. What is the gift of righteousness and when do you receive it? The gift of righteousness is a new spirit, and it becomes yours when you are born again. You do not earn it; there's no way you can be any more righteous in your spirit after you are saved. Your soul and your body, however, are another story, because nothing happens to them when you are saved.

As we saw in Hebrews above, when we yield to the discipline of the Lord, it produces the peaceable fruits of righteousness, which are *"love, joy, peace, patience, kindness, goodness, faithfulness, gentleness, [and] self-control"* (Galatians 5:22–23). And if, indeed, a person received a new spirit from the Father of spirits—or he claims that he has—but there's no evidence of these fruits in his life, then I would question whether he ever received that gift. Jesus requires fruit. John 15 tells us the Father is the Vine-dresser, Jesus is the Vine, and we are the branches. Where does the fruit grow? On the branches, and every branch that doesn't bear fruit is pruned away. The supply of the branch is the Vine, and the Father is the Gardener; He's the Father of spirits; the One who trains us to yield the fruits of righteousness. If your spirit man is not producing fruit, then your soul man is not saved, because the requirement for a saved soul is one of these fruits. Luke 21:19 (NKJV) says, *"By your patience possess your souls."* If you're yielding to the Father of spirits, who disciplines us, then you will produce the fruit of patience, which will enable you to take total dominion over the soul man (the mind, will, and emotions). With this fruit, you have the ability to take control of the soul man. According to 1 Peter 1:9, the saving of your soul is the end—the goal—of your faith! When you take hold of your soul, then the real you, the spirit man, and your soul will take the flesh and crucify it. That's how we walk in the Spirit!

> **When you take hold of your soul, then the real you, the spirit man, and your soul will take the flesh and crucify it. That's how we walk in the Spirit!**

Remember the three types of people who walk the earth, according to 1 Corinthians 2:14:

> *But a natural man does not accept the things of the Spirit of God, for they are foolishness to him; and he cannot understand them, because they are spiritually appraised.*

1. **The Natural Man** (the "dead walking"): He cannot understand spiritual things because his spirit is dead. God hasn't yet fathered a new spirit in him, so he is incapable of spiritual knowledge.

2. **The Carnal Man:**

> *However, brethren, I could not talk to you as to spiritual [men], but as to nonspiritual [men of the flesh, in whom the carnal nature predominates], as to mere infants [in the new life] in Christ [unable to talk yet!]. I fed you with milk, not solid food, for you were not yet strong enough [to be ready for it], for you are still [unspiritual].*
>
> (1 Corinthians 3:1–3 AMP)

This church was speaking in tongues, but they were unspiritual. Speaking in tongues is important—but if the fruit of patience isn't operating in a person to the extent that he can possess his own soul, then he is carnal. He's on his way to heaven, but he is going to have a horrible time getting there, because he is going to be fighting his flesh all the way! If you don't possess your soul man, it will team up with your flesh against your spirit. The degree of authority that you have over your body is the same degree of authority you have in the Spirit. Paul describes carnal Christians as *"mere (unchanged) men"* (1 Corinthians 3:3 AMP). These Christians received a new spirit, but because they were not able to possess their soul man, they were living as if nothing had happened. There was no fruit in their lives.

3. **The Spiritual Man:** He tries—examines, investigates, inquires, questions, and discerns—all things, yet is put on trial or judged by no one. (See 1 Corinthians 2:15.) When you are a spiritual man or woman, you will see into other people, but they won't be able to see into you. You will be able to see into

situations in which others cannot. You will have the mind of Christ. Scripture tells us that there is no condemnation (no judgment of guilt) for those who are in Christ Jesus—the ones who follow the dictates of the Spirit rather than the dictates of the flesh. (See Romans 8:1, 4.)

The Holy Spirit is in your spirit; He's dictating, but do you hear Him? Or are you listening to the body? The body is a terrible dictator! What do you have to do to follow after the dictates of the flesh? Nothing! Get up, eat, work, sleep! I guarantee you, you will be flesh-led the rest of your life if you follow worldly dictates! Paul said, "*I keep under my body*" (1 Corinthians 9:27 KJV). His spirit man possessed his body and kept it in subjection to the Holy Spirit rather than allow it to follow the dictates of the flesh.

Romans 8:2 (NKJV) says, "*For the law of the Spirit of life in Christ Jesus has made me free from the law of sin and death.*" The law of the Spirit of life (LSL) is greater than the law of sin and death (LSD)! Every day when you wake up, the choice is in front of you: LSL on the right and LSD on the left. You may say, "Well, LSD is acid!" Yes, and it belongs in the law of sin and death! So does rage, abuse, and disease. The law of sin and death is anything that tries to kill you. It's really easy to distinguish between the two. Jesus said, "*I have come that they may have life...*" (John 10:10 NKJV). On the other hand, the thief comes to do what? Steal, kill, and destroy (see John 10:10)—that's the law of sin and death. So, the question is this: What's happening in your soul? What are you looking at? What are you dwelling on? What were your dominant thoughts today? That's what you're constructing.

For those who are according to the flesh and are controlled by its unholy desires set their minds on and pursue those things which gratify the flesh, but those who are according to the Spirit and are controlled by the desires of the Spirit set their minds on and seek those things which gratify the [Holy] Spirit.   (Romans 8:5 AMP)

Whether you walk in the Spirit or walk in the flesh will depend upon what you put into your mind at any given moment! So fill your mind with the Word of God.

6

CONVERSATIONS WITH
THE SOUL

Whether you're a sports fan or not, if you love Jesus, you will rejoice in the following story about the Baltimore Ravens.

"They were supposed to lose to the [Denver] Broncos on Saturday [January 12, 2013]. They were done when they got the ball on their own 23-yard line with 1:09 left in regulation, trailing 35–28. Then quarterback Joe Flacco...heaved a long pass to receiver Jacoby Jones, who grabbed the ball from the frosty air and ran to the end zone for a 70-yard touchdown that tied the game. They survived an entire overtime until they hit the winning field goal less than two minutes into the second overtime. And all of it seems so much like something that is bigger than them all.

"All week [Ray] Lewis had challenged his teammates. He told them not to listen to the voices outside their practice facility in the Baltimore suburbs. He called on them to remember all the injuries they endured in a season where starter after starter went down. He told them he had a dream they would bond together and fight through significant odds and win a championship.

"Then before they left the locker room on Saturday afternoon he quoted from the Bible.

"'No weapon formed against us shall prosper,' he said."At halftime he brought the players together, made them touch each other and repeat the same phrase.'"The whole day I just needed my team to keep reciting: "No weapon,"' he said later. 'The energy is crazy, the emotions are crazy, but to stay the course the way this team stayed the course, I tip my hat off to my team.'

"The players do not speak openly about Lewis' impending retirement and the motivation it appears to have rendered. They say this run is bigger than him. Head coach John Harbaugh agreed on Saturday, pinching his fingers about an inch apart when asked to quantify how much Lewis' retirement is driving them. He too spoke of the Bible. He said he realized that talking about this will make people uncomfortable but he spoke as if Lewis' expressions of faith has become a unifying element in a room that a few weeks before might have been filled with doubt.

"'There is spirituality in here,' Harbaugh said. 'I can't describe it.'

"Perhaps such things are said on nights like Saturday, when victory is pulled from certain defeat. But there is also no doubt that the booming presence of Lewis stomping around the locker room has brought this team to life again. If Lewis is going to quote scripture, the Ravens are more than happy to buy in."[21]

Now, you don't find that kind of testimony much among professional sportsmen, and I rejoice in it.

Ray Lewis got his entire team to speak faith-filled words to their souls. Their bodies had to obey those commands on the

---

21. Les Carpenter, "Ray Lewis, Peyton Manning Share Special Moment After Broncos-Ravens Playoff Classic," *Yahoo Sports* (13 January 2013), http://sports.yahoo.com/news/nfl--ray-lewis--peyton-manning-share-special-moment-after-broncos-ravens-playoff-classic-062005410.html.

football field. Their spirits and souls dominated their bodies and enabled them to win the game.

They have my vote, because I know that Ray Lewis loves Jesus! If you don't get up in the morning commanding your soul, then your mind, will, and emotions are going to hit you in the face all day long. If you don't get up and command your soul, then your soul will command you. Psalm 103 is a psalm of commanding the soul. What the Lord showed me about Psalm 103 is that David was having some struggles with his soul man. That's why this Psalm starts out with a command: *"Bless the LORD, O my soul"* (Psalm 103:1). He's not asking his soul; he's commanding his soul.

> **If you don't get up in the morning commanding your soul, then your mind, will, and emotions are going to hit you in the face all day long. If you don't get up and command your soul, then your soul will command you.**

If you have never done this, then you ought to. Your spirit man has to be in charge so it can take authority over your soul. You have to give your soul verbal commands, like this: "Bless the Lord, and all that is within me, bless His holy name!" Unlike your spirit, your soul will not remember what God has done for you, so you *must* remind it. Notice the next verse: *"Bless the LORD, O my soul, and forget none of His benefits"* (Psalm 103:2). David's not asking his soul; he's commanding his soul: "Soul, you will *not* forget the following benefits!" What benefits? The Lord is the one...

1. *"Who pardons all your iniquities"* (Psalm 103:3).
2. *"Who heals all your diseases"* (verse 3).
3. *"Who redeems your life from the pit"* (verse 4).
4. *"Who crowns you with lovingkindness and compassion"* (verse 4).
5. *"Who satisfies your years with good things, so that your youth is renewed like the eagle"* (verse 5).

What kind of conversation are you having with your soul? Charles Spurgeon found a dear sister who was starving to death. She had been a caregiver for a very wealthy family most of her life, and in their will was an allotment for a home and food to set her up for the rest of her life. But she didn't know the benefits—she was starving to death. On the wall, Spurgeon saw a plaque of the will. He asked this lady, "Ma'am, would you mind if I take this to the authorities?" The lady replied, "No, this is so very precious. It came from…"

See what I'm talking about? Her answer was on the wall; the benefits were there, but she was dying. Likewise, you can die with the benefits that were paid on the cross. *You must talk to your soul!* I talk to mine. The flu used to wipe me out just like everyone else. Two weeks—bam! But now my health is better than it's ever been, and it gets better every day. I live in a human body just like you.

The sister in the Spurgeon account finally allowed him to take that plaque to the authorities, and everything changed because of the benefits that were there all along. Hosea 4:6 says, *"My people are destroyed for lack of knowledge."* Knowledge exists in the soul man—in the mind, the will, and the emotions.

Just as David commanded his soul, so we should speak verbal commands, such as, "Soul, listen to me!" Psalm 45:1 says that the *"tongue is the pen of a ready writer."* Your tongue is so important. Do you remember the woman with the issue of blood in Mark 5? She was dying. She'd had internal bleeding for twelve years. She heard about Jesus but didn't say, "I'm going to wait for Him to come to my house." She would've died! Instead, she told herself, "If I can but touch His clothes, I shall be whole!" (See Matthew 9:21.) She talked to her soul, and she kept talking to her soul until she began to move. She didn't walk to Jesus. How do we know this? Because she touched the hem of His garment. (See Matthew 9:20.) She was on the ground. She spoke commands to the degree that, somehow, she got to Jesus. And faith pulled the power out.

Take a moment and say, "Soul, listen to me: God satisfies *my* mouth—not the preacher's mouth, not the evangelist's mouth— *my* mouth, with good things, so that *my* youth is renewed as the eagles'. Many of you are eagles, but you've been living like chickens. I have a little book titled *Soar as the Eagles*. There are a couple of passages in it that I'd like to share with you. Read this short passage:

> One spring day a boy was playing in the woods when suddenly he spotted something that looked like a nest. As he crept closer he saw it was a bird's nest with only one egg in it. Instinctively, he looked around but he didn't see any birds flying above him. The boy decided to take the egg home.
>
> After showing the egg to his parents, he placed it in the chicken coop. (He hoped a chicken would sit on the egg until it hatched.) Finally, the day came for the hatching, and excitedly the boy ran and got his parents to come see the baby bird. But then came the revelation: The boy's father looked at the baby bird and told his son it was an eagle.

As the eagle grew, the boy's father helped clip its wings. The eagle seemed content in the barnyard with all of the chickens. Summer came, and the boy and his father became busy and forgot about the eagle. The father forgot to keep the eagle's wings clipped. No one noticed that the eagle grew more restless with each passing day.

With the change of seasons it was inevitable that a summer storm would come, too. As the wind moaned and whipped through the barnyard, all the chickens began to hurry and scurry to find shelter. But not the eagle. The eagle stood with its wings spread out, looking into the sky. There, amid the pelting rain and lightning flashes was another eagle soaring with the storm.

Just then a gust of wind arose. The wind filled the young eagle's wings, enabling it to lift up from the ground and soar high into the sky with the other eagle. At last, soaring with another eagle, the orphaned bird knew its purpose in life.

Like the eagle, we too can learn our purpose in life once we know the great love our heavenly Father has for us.[22]

There are some of you who have had your wings clipped by hurt and lies; but there's an anointing for growing them back: Will you receive it?

There are a lot of eagles in God's army who are content to hang with the chickens. While chickens run from stormy weather; eagles soar into it. Would you be an eagle in God's army?

Your soul is not going to get saved in an instant. It's going to take time to speak commands. It takes me almost thirty minutes each day just to speak forth God's words over me. And that's

---

22. Sheryl Lynn Hill, *Soar as the Eagle* (Uhrichsville, OH: Barbour Publishing, 2000).

not counting the hours and hours of speaking in tongues. Why? Because my soul doesn't know any better. Likewise, your soul doesn't know any better; so you have to command it. fly, an eagle also spends up to an hour a day preening its feathers to be ready to fly. Does the Bible say, "Those who wait on the Lord will mount up with wings as chickens"? No! *They will mount up with wings like **eagles**"* (Isaiah 40:31).

Here are just a few things an eagle does every day:

Eagles spend hours each day preening each of their feathers, which can number up to 1,200! This has a similar affect to steam cleaning. Likewise, each day, you've got to have the breath of the Holy Spirit; you can't live on yesterday's anointing. What does this mean for us as believers? What can we draw from this? You've got to get up and get cleaned! You've got to speak to your own soul and command it according to the dictates of the Spirit. Because, if you don't speak to your soul, it will certainly speak to you! It will say, "You good-for-nothing!" "Look what happened last week!" "You might as well throw in the towel!" "You're going under!" "You're not going to make it!" "You're going to die!"

> You've got to speak to your own soul and command it according to the dictates of the Spirit. Because, if you don't speak to your soul, it will certainly speak to you!

How do you stop that ungodly chatter? You command it to stop! "Soul, stop! I'm not going to listen to you, telling me I'm good-for-nothing and a failure! I'm not going to listen to your nonsense about dying!" God's Word says, *"I will not die, but live"* (Psalm 118:17)! Do you know that some people have to be talked out of dying before they can be healed? You know, nothing just happens. Show me a miracle, and I will show you great persistence! That's why Scripture says to fight the good fight of faith. (See 1 Timothy 6:12.) There is a fight to faith, but it is not with the enemy; Jesus has already defeated him. The fight is to stay in faith! The fight is to speak to your soul.

Now, once an eagle's feathers are restored, it is ready to soar to the sky. You mean the eagle doesn't just get up and take off soaring? No. Every single morning, he goes through a cleansing, renewal process…and then he soars! Sometimes the eagle molts and has to regrow its feathers; other times, it has to sharpen its beak. In a similar fashion, there are times when God calls us to a season of renewal. That's why He often compares us to the eagle. So, are you going to run with the chickens or are you going to soar with the eagles?

Furthermore, the eagle secretes an oily liquid on its feathers, making them waterproof. Do you get before the Lord every morning and say, "Wash me with Your blood. Cleanse me, Lord. Are there any unhealthy old ties or wicked ways in me? Then cleanse me, Lord. Fill me fresh with Your mighty Holy Spirit. I want a fresh infilling. I can't go on yesterday's anointing; I need an oil change!"

The oily liquid is very advantageous to an eagle's faring in wet weather and even in hunting. When the bird dives into the water after its prey, it's feathers are not weighed down with water, endangering its ability to fly. We, too, must renew ourselves daily before the Lord, or we will be weighed down with the things of the world. Without those necessary quiet times, the problems of this life will bring on anxieties and fears, which will slow us down. Worry renders us powerless; faith begins to falter.

Fretting often springs from a determination to get our own way. But there is no "Burger King" Christianity. That chain knows virtually nothing about a king or a kingdom. You can't have it your way; it's God's way—the King's decree. It's not a smorgasbord or a cafeteria. Get up in the morning praising God, and just watch how He will order your day.

7

SPIRITUAL AMMO FOR THE SOUL

In the previous chapter, we looked at Psalm 103 and discussed the importance of giving your soul verbal commands. Now, it's not your place to give my soul commands, and it's not my place to give your soul commands. Although, there are a lot of busybodies out there: They are busy with other people's lives but not with their own! You've got to be busy taking command of your own body and soul!

> *But the news about Him was spreading even farther, and large crowds were gathering to hear Him and to be healed of their sicknesses. But Jesus Himself would often slip away to the wilderness and pray.* (Luke 5:15–16)

Luke 5:15 tells us how multitudes of people came together to hear Jesus teach, and to be healed by Him. "Well," you say, "Jesus just stayed with the crowd, and the power of God was there!" No, not really! What did He do immediately after He ministered? "[He] *would often slip away to the wilderness and pray.*" This is why He stayed anointed. He came out of His quiet times and then performed the miracles. One translation says, "[He] *often withdrew to lonely places and prayed*" (Luke 5:16 NIV).

I'm learning about those lonely places. It's lonely to shut yourself up from humanity for hours and pray and fast. But is it worth it? Oh, absolutely, yes! It's worth it to see God's anointing, to see God's power. Jesus didn't get His team to do it for Him—He did it, and we need to be people of prayer, just like Jesus.

Does prayer and fasting have anything to do with the soul man? It has a lot to do with it. There's a whole lot that goes into getting your soul saved. If you're having problems tarrying in prayer, here's a passage for you:

> I humbled my soul with fasting, and my prayer kept return-
> ing to my bosom. (Psalm 35:13)

These are David's words, and this is why he stayed anointed and in the "flow" of the Spirit. If you're struggling with prayer, then maybe you need to inform your soul man that he's not the boss. And if you start denying your soul man some things, well, all the better! Your spirit should be running the show, so you are giving your soul man—your mind, your will, and your emotions—commands: "Settle down, soul man, settle down!" Remember the benefits of God in Psalm 103:2–5? Now, your soul man will forget those benefits, so it's the job of the spirit man to constantly keep them before the soul man. Talk to your soul. You can't flow in the Spirit if your soul man's in charge! When Absalom rose up against his own father, David cried out, *"Many are saying of my soul, There is no deliverance for him in God"* (Psalm 3:2). But then he began to declare, *"But You, O LORD, are a shield about me, my glory, and the One who lifts my head"* (Psalm 3:3). David commanded his soul to praise God for His favor and help!

Let's look at some more psalms dealing with the soul man:

And my soul is greatly dismayed; but You, O LORD—how long? Return, O LORD, rescue my soul; save me because of Your lovingkindness. (Psalm 6:3–4)

Arise, O LORD, confront him, bring him low; deliver my soul from the wicked with Your sword. (Psalm 17:13)

The law of the LORD is perfect, restoring the soul; the testimony of the LORD is sure, making wise the simple. (Psalm 19:7)

To keep your spirit man in charge, you've got to keep God's Word before you. You've got to be looking at it. You've got to be hearing it. I woke up this morning and listened to the Word. Why? Because I made the choice that my soul man was going to hear the Word. The law of the Lord will convert the soul man.

He restores my soul. (Psalm 23:3)

Just say this: "Soul, listen to me: You're being restored!" You've got to give your soul commands every day. It's easy to do when you're gathered together with other believers, but when you wake up in the morning, it may be a challenge.

To You, O LORD, I lift up my soul. (Psalm 25:1)

Who's lifting the soul up? "I"—the spirit man—the real you!

Guard my soul and deliver me; do not let me be ashamed, for I take refuge in You. (Psalm 25:20)

You have turned for me my mourning into dancing; you have loosed my sackcloth and girded me with gladness, that my soul may sing praise to You and not be silent. (Psalm 30:11–12)

Behold, the eye of the LORD *is on those who fear Him, on those who hope for His lovingkindness, to deliver their soul from death and to keep them alive in famine. Our soul waits for the* LORD; *He is our help and our shield.*

(Psalm 33:18–20)

Tell your soul this: "No matter what's happening on this earth, my soul will be protected from death, and I will always have plenty to eat and drink."

That's what I was doing today. It took a lot longer today than usual for the anointing to come. So what did I do? I just kept on. What do you do when your soul doesn't want to respond? You should keep doing what the Lord says and keep waiting for Him to come…and He'll show up.

Remember that Luke 21:19 tells us to possess our own souls in patience. This ties in with what we discussed in chapter 5, "The Three Types of Man and How They Affect the Spirit." God fathered our spirits, and inside of them are nine seeds that produce nine fruit: love, joy, peace, patience, kindness, goodness, faithfulness, gentleness, and self-control.

God fathered our spirits, and inside of them are nine seeds that produce nine fruit: love, joy, peace, patience, kindness, goodness, faithfulness, gentleness, and self-control.

Let's camp here for just a minute. Consider the fruit "faithfulness." When that's in us, we won't say, "Well, I'll be in church if the creek don't rise." If the Word is in you, that won't be coming

out of your mouth! Why? Because the Word says, "The waters
will not overflow me. Though I walk through the fire, I will not
be burned." (See Isaiah 43:2.) You have that authority, but you
must walk in faithfulness to activate it. Then fruit of patience
will possess the soul man and take authority over it. God put the
seed of faithfulness in your spirit man to be watered and grown.

Back to the Psalms:

> *My soul shall make its boast in the Lord; the humble will*
> *hear it and rejoice.*   (Psalm 34:2)

Say that every day!

> *The Lord redeems the soul of His servants.* (Psalm 34:22)

You want to know how to get your soul saved? Get a hold
of these verses, say them with your mouth, give your soul
commands.

> *As the deer pants for the water brooks, so my soul pants for*
> *You, O God. My soul thirsts for God, for the living God; when*
> *shall I come and appear before God?*   (Psalm 42:1–2)

> *Why are you in despair, O my soul?*   (Psalm 42:5)

You mean, when I'm having a low moment and my emotions
are all over the place, this is what I'm supposed to do? Yes, get
out this Word and speak it aloud!

> *Why are you in despair, O my soul? And why have you*
> *become disturbed within me? Hope in God, for I shall yet*
> *praise Him, the help of my countenance and my God.*
>   (Psalm 42:11)

Behold, God is my helper; the LORD *is the sustainer of my soul.*   (Psalm 54:4)

Glory to God! I don't know what's going on the next block over, but I know what's going on at the McManus residence: The Lord God is our helper; the Lord is the sustainer of our soul!

You've got some ammo now. You want to know what to do when the soul man tries to go haywire? Write down every one of these verses and put them where you can get a hold of them quickly. Then speak them to your soul!

8

CHECKS AND BALANCES
FOR THE SOUL

You have to talk to your soul. You may have to talk to it several times a day. I've already had some strong talks with mine today. I don't trust my soul—I command it. I don't trust my mind—I command it. I put God's thoughts into my mind. I am a spirit; I have a soul (mind, will, emotions), and I live in a body. My mind is made up of thoughts and feelings, and, according to 1 Peter 1:9, the end or the goal of my faith is the saving of my soul.

Tell your soul, "You're getting saved. You don't have any choice in the matter." As we've been learning, sometimes you just have to get bold with your soul. Either you'll tell your soul what to do, or your soul will tell you what to do or what your day's going to be like! Every day, the same options are there.

Let's look at some Scriptures, some ammunition for the soul—and particularly the mind.

> [Moses] *said to them, "Take to your heart all the words with which I am warning you today, which you shall command your sons to observe carefully, even all the words of this law."* (Deuteronomy 32:46)

This Scripture instructs us to set our minds and hearts on the Word of God and to teach it to our children. You create the mind-set that you ponder every day. If you are diligent to focus on the Word, you will keep your soul man in check!

When the enemy rose up against God's people as they were rebuilding the walls of their city, Nehemiah said,

> I looked [them over] and rose up and said to the nobles and officials and the other people, Do not be afraid of the enemy; [earnestly] remember the Lord and imprint Him [on your minds].   (Nehemiah 4:14 AMP)

I want to tell you that when God is imprinted on your mind, fear will not be able to enter your life. Fear of lack, fear of destruction, fear of death—they will not have dominion over you!

Let's look at Psalm 103 again. This is a psalm of commanding your soul; we covered the first part of it a little while ago. Verses 10–12 (AMP) read,

> He has not dealt with us after our sins nor rewarded us according to our iniquities. For as the heavens are high above the earth, so great are His mercy **and** lovingkindness toward those who reverently and worshipfully fear Him. As far as the east is from the west, so far has He removed our transgressions from us.

He has removed our sins from us "as far as the east is from the west." If the enemy is trying to beat you over the head for something that is already under the blood, stand up, face the east, and proclaim, "Father, I know Your Word says that as far as the east is from the west, that's how far You have removed my transgressions from me! I am free! I am clean! East never meets west, and my sins will never meet me again! In Jesus' name!"

God's kingdom rules over all. (See Psalm 103:19 KJV.) You can face everything that comes your way today with boldness. You need not worry or be fretful or fearful, because God's throne is the highest level of all authority; He rules over everything that comes your way today.

> ## Remind your soul, as you speak to it, that God's angels are right here, performing, moving, and doing on your behalf as you voice God's Word. You are protected. You are saved. No destruction will ever come near you.

Psalm 103:20 (AMP) says, "*Bless (affectionately, gratefully praise) the Lord, you His angels, you mighty ones who do His commandments, hearkening to the voice of His word.*" Remind your soul, as you speak to it, that God's angels are right here, performing, moving, and doing on your behalf as you voice God's Word. You are protected. You are saved. No destruction will ever come near you. You drive with angelic escorts. You arise every morning with angels around you. Wherever you go, God's angels are with you, and they hearken to the voice of God's Word!

> *Bless (affectionately, gratefully praise) the Lord, all you His hosts, you His ministers who do His pleasure. Bless the Lord, all His works in all places of His dominion."*
> (Psalm 103:21–22 AMP)

What does "*all His works in all places of His dominion*" mean? It means that everywhere you go, you are carrying the kingdom. God's kingdom rules over all. So wherever you go, you have the right to take dominion. Tell your soul, "Wherever I go, whatever I face—whether it's robbery, whether it's a riot—I bring the kingdom, and the kingdom rules over it. It is subject to His dominion." Until Jesus returns and rules from the New Jerusalem, you and I carry the kingdom, and, wherever we go, the kingdom goes. This psalm ends the way it begins: *"Bless (affectionately, gratefully praise) the Lord, O my soul!"* (Psalm 103:22).Here is some more good ammunition:

> *The mind of the prudent is ever getting knowledge, and the ear of the wise is ever seeking (inquiring for and craving) knowledge.* (Proverbs 18:15 AMP)

I don't let whatever is coming out through the television, or whatever some group is saying, to get into my mind. I am the custodian of my mind, and I have made the decision to put God's knowledge into my mind. *You* are the custodian of your mind. Tell your soul, "I make the quality decision to put God's knowledge in my mind. I don't accept something just because it preaches good. I demand book, chapter, and verse!" Just because something sounds good doesn't mean it IS good!

> *"Teacher, which is the great commandment in the Law?" And He said to him, "You shall love the Lord your God with all your heart, and with all your soul, and with all your mind." This is the great and foremost commandment."* (Matthew 22:36–38)

It's a command to love God with all your mind, but how do you do that? By saturating your mind with God's Word. *You* have to do it. Whatever you do when you get up in the morning—whether watching TV or reading the newspaper or praying and studying God's Word—is up to you. You're the custodian of your mind, your soul, and your body, just as I'm the custodian of mine. I'm commanded to love God with my mind. Most of the time, when I get up in the morning, my mind doesn't want to love Him. If you wake up in the morning and you've got contrary thoughts to the Philippians 4:8 Test—the six criteria that every thought must pass in order to be good building material for your mind—chuck them! Remember, you are commanded to love God with your mind, so if you embrace bad thoughts, you are in disobedience. You have to constantly chuck out those bad thoughts and entertain good ones. This may require you to change what you allow into your mind.

> ## Remember, you are commanded to love God with your mind, so if you embrace bad thoughts, you are in disobedience. You have to constantly chuck out those bad thoughts and entertain good ones.

If you're having problems understanding the Word, pray this Scripture:

> *Then He [thoroughly] opened up their minds to understand the Scriptures.*　　　　(Luke 24:45 AMP)

Thank God for opening up your mind completely, so that you can understand His Word and love Him as you are commanded to love Him. Now look at Romans 8:5 (AMP), which says,

> *For those who are according to the flesh and are controlled by its unholy desires set their minds on and pursue those things which gratify the flesh, but those who are according*

to the Spirit and are controlled by the desires of the Spirit set their minds on and seek those things which gratify the [Holy] Spirit.

Here is the great dividing line between the spiritual Christian and the flesh-ruled in the body of Christ. One simple fact separates them: *"Those who are according to the flesh…set their minds on and pursue those things which gratify the flesh."* "Well, it's a movie," you say, "and there's going to be some adultery, some bad language…." You know, I'm not the custodian of your mind. *You* are! The problem is in the head! What are you going to set your mind on?

What does *"pursue"* mean? To go after something. What do you pursue? Also, how do you love God with your mind? *By watching what you put in it.*

First Corinthians 14:20 instructs us not to be children, immature in our thinking or thoughts. We are told to continue to *"be babes in [matters of] evil"* (AMP) and mature men in our minds.

Furthermore, we should conduct ourselves in such a way that our lives are worthy of the gospel of Christ.

Only conduct yourselves in a manner worthy of the gospel of Christ, so that whether I come and see you or remain absent, I will hear of you that you are standing firm in one spirit, with one mind striving together for the faith of the gospel. (Philippians 1:27)

It's your job to conduct yourself. Nobody can do it for you. So here's the question: Would you live the way you're living if the whole church were around? That's what Paul is saying in the verse of Scripture above: "Whether I'm with you or absent." You know that old saying "When the cat's away, the mice will play." I'm going to tell you, God is never away! And He doesn't need night vision goggles. Scripture says that the night and the day are the same to God. (See Psalm 139:12.) So God sees every bit of what you do when no one else is around—whether in the daytime or at night.

Again, you are the custodian of your mind. Don't trust your mind. Don't serve it; make it serve you, the real you—your spirit man.

> *If any of you is deficient in wisdom, let him ask of the giving God [Who gives] to everyone liberally and ungrudgingly, without reproaching or faultfinding, and it will be given him. Only it must be in faith that he asks with no wavering (no hesitating, and no doubting). For the one who wavers (hesitates, doubts) is like the billowing surge out at sea that is blown hither and thither and tossed by the wind. For truly, let not such a person imagine that he will receive anything [he asks for] from the Lord, [for being as he is] a man of two minds (hesitating, dubious, irresolute), [he is] unstable and unreliable and uncertain about everything [he thinks, feels, decides].*   (James 1:5–8 AMP)

How do you know if you have two minds? You hesitate, you waver, you doubt. A person with no integrity is a person of two minds. He will tell you he'll be there, but he won't show up. Why? Because his other mind took over. The Bible says to be single-minded. Having the mind of Christ is single-mindedness.

As you can see, the saved soul affects everything—what we say and what we do. It makes us people of our word—whether it's convenient or not, whether we feel like it or not. Remember, feelings are in the mind, or the soul. So, when we get up in the morning, we must set our thoughts—or fix our minds—on the things above.

9

HOW TO HAVE
A HEALTHY BODY
AND SOUL

Let's review: What do you do with bad studs, or thoughts? Chuck them! Isaiah 26:3 (KJV) says, *"Thou wilt keep him in perfect peace, whose mind is stayed* [formed, framed] *on thee."* You could say it like this: "You, God, will keep me in perfect peace, because my mind will dwell on only good studs from God's Word, and form and frame God's will for my life." You need to know the Scriptures on your soul so you can dwell on them and speak them over your life. You have to get a hold of the the following nugget Scriptures. They may be small, but they pack a lot of power!:

> *The LORD will protect you from all evil; He will keep your soul.* (Psalm 121:7)

> *I wait for the LORD, my soul does wait, and in His word do I hope.* (Psalm 130:5)

> *Surely I have composed and quieted my soul.* (Psalm 131:2)

Who is *"I"*? The spirit man. Remember, you are a spirit, and you have a soul, but your soul's not the real "you." You live in a body, but the body isn't the real you, either. If your body says you're sick, that's not you. It's important that you know this. Since your body's not you, then you have authority over it. And the degree that your soul is saved will be the degree that your body will be living in health, because 3 John 2 (kjv) says, *"Beloved, I wish above all things that thou mayest prosper and be in health, even as thy soul prospereth."* You can compose and quiet your soul because you—the real you—is where God lives.

> *On the day I called, You answered me; You made me bold*
> *with strength in my soul.*   (Psalm 138:3)

> *Bring my soul out of prison, so that I may give thanks to*
> *Your name; the righteous will surround me, for You will*
> *deal bountifully with me.*   (Psalm 142:7)

If you've come to a place where you feel your mind, your emotions, is under attack, and you feel like you've been put in a prison, Psalm 142:7 is a good Scripture for you. If you feel like your soul is in prison, there's an anointing that will bring you right out of it.

> *Let me hear Your lovingkindness in the morning; for I trust*
> *in You; teach me the way in which I should walk; for to You*
> *I lift up my soul.*   (Psalm 143:8)

We should hear God's lovingkindness in the morning and lift up our souls to Him. That's how we all should start each day in the morning, saying, "God, I lift up my soul to You." We're lifting up our mind, our emotions, and our will to Him, and that will carry us through the day.

Here's another Scripture if your soul is in trouble:

For the sake of Your name, O LORD, revive me. In Your righteousness bring my soul out of trouble. (Psalm 143:11)

And another direct soul command:

Bless the LORD, O my soul!   (Psalm 103:1)

We need to get in this mind-set and start praising Him more. It doesn't have a thing to do with feelings or anything else. You're commanding your soul. If you take authority over your soul, your feelings will line up. If you're waiting for your feelings to just get in line, you're going to miss out on many, many blessings. God wants us to believe first, and then feelings will come. Believe first, and feelings will follow!

Let's jump over to the New Testament for a little bit:

And the very God of peace sanctify you wholly; and I pray God your whole spirit and soul and body be preserved blameless unto the coming of our Lord Jesus Christ.
                    (1 Thessalonians 5:23 KJV)

This is another scriptural proof of the triune nature of man. Here we find Paul's prayer for the brethren in Thessalonica, that their spirits and souls and bodies would be blameless for the coming of the Lord. God's will is that you be whole—spirit, soul, and body—and in that order, too: spirit first, then soul, and then body.

For the word of God is quick [alive], and powerful, and sharper than any twoedged sword, piercing even to the dividing asunder of soul and spirit, and of the joints and marrow, and is a discerner of the thoughts and intents of the heart.   (Hebrews 4:12 KJV)

The hope we have in the Lord is an anchor of the soul.

Now faith is the assurance of things hoped for, the conviction of things not seen.   (Hebrews 11:1)

This hope we have as an anchor of the soul, a hope both sure and steadfast.   (Hebrews 6:19)

Faith is in the spirit realm; hope is the soul realm. Hope is desire, an emotion. It's what you're reaching for. Faith is what grabs hold of that and causes it to become a reality. So, for faith even to work, you've got to have hope. Hope needs faith, and faith needs hope.

Faith is what grabs hold of that and causes it to become a reality. So, for faith even to work, you've got to have hope. Hope needs faith, and faith needs hope.

You're reading this book because you hope to get something meaningful out of it. This Scripture illustrates, through the lives of great biblical characters, that hope truly is the anchor of the soul. Without that anchor, your soul will be carried to-and-fro like a boat on a turbulent ocean of your emotions. Hope anchors the soul. Each day, tell yourself, "I will get a hold of what God promised me in the Scriptures, and I will make it my soul's desire, so that I can see my body well, my finances met, and my family restored. Hope will anchor my soul man!"

But My righteous one shall live by faith; and if he shrinks back, My soul has no pleasure in him. But we are not of

those who shrink back to destruction, but of those who have
faith to the preserving of the soul.   (Hebrews 10:38–39)

This Scripture talks about the just, who live by faith…and those who fall away from the faith, in whom God says He has *"no pleasure."* Tell your soul, "I am not of the group that draws back from the things of God into perdition but of them who believe to the saving of the soul."

We covered this next Scripture, but it's a good one to review:

Wherefore lay apart all filthiness and superfluity of naugh-
tiness, and receive with meekness the engrafted word, which
is able to save your souls.   (James 1:21 KJV)

Your soul will not be saved if you don't stay in the Word! It's directly related to the amount of the Word that is in you.

Since you have in obedience to the truth purified your souls
for a sincere love of the brethren, fervently love one another
from the heart.   (1 Peter 1:22)

This Scripture explains how we can purify our souls: by obeying the truth of God's Word, which gives us a sincere love for one another. Your soul is pure if you not only hear the Word but also do it!

Beloved, I urge you as aliens and strangers to abstain from
fleshly lusts which wage war against the soul.
(1 Peter 2:11)

We are instructed to abstain from fleshly lusts that war against the soul. Make it a point to tell your soul, "I will not engage in, look at, listen to, turn on, or pay for anything that's going to open the door to fleshly lusts that will war against my soul, which is in the process of being saved."Did you know that one of the names of the Lord is the shepherd and bishop of ours? (See 1 Peter 2:25 KJV.) Now, if He is the shepherd and bishop of your mind, your will, and your emotions, you won't be giving pieces of your mind away. Rather, you will be dedicating them to serving Jesus!

Ephesians 4:23 tells us to be *"renewed in the spirit of your mind."* What the Lord showed me is that, in order for this to happen, the spirit realm has got to be preeminent over the mind realm; and one way that is done is through praying in other tongues.

Dr. Carl R. Peterson published an article on the medical benefits of speaking in tongues,[23] and Simon Yaps, who has spent years studying tongues, commented on it:

> First, a caveat: I am not a Charismatic, but I was fortunate to receive the gift of tongues without anyone laying his or her hands on me.
>
> Secondly, this note is not only for people who do not believe in the gift of tongues but those who don't understand why God would give such a gift as His first gift to the church, and whether it is relevant today.
>
> I ask you to read it with an open mind. My intention is to bring praise to God for such a gift and pray that those who have received such a gift use it for His glory.

•••

God has made provision for you and me to be whole, to be well and to have access to His healing process. There is a study that has been done by Dr. Carl Peterson, M.D. (the husband of author and evangelist Vicki Jamison-Peterson).

---

23. Dr. Carl R. Peterson, *Medical Facts About Speaking in Tongues.*

This study reveals that there is an available healing power that can be released from our own bodies for our own benefit. Dr. Carl Peterson worked on this study at ORU in Tulsa, Oklahoma, a few years ago. Being a brain specialist, he was doing research on what the relationship was between the brain and praying, or speaking, in tongues. Some amazing things were discovered.

Through research and testing, he found that as we pray in the Spirit, or worship in the Spirit (our heavenly language), there is activity that begins to take place in the brain.

As we engage in our heavenly language, the brain releases two chemical secretions that are directed into our immune system, [giving it a 35 to 40 percent boost]. This promotes healing within our bodies. Amazingly, this secretion is triggered from a part of the brain that has no other apparent activity in humans, and is only activated by our Spirit-led prayer and worship.[24]

Dr. Carl Peterson wrote this in response to an inquiry on the relationship between extended periods of praying in tongues and joyful laughter, and brain activity:

I have had a number of inquiries concerning the efficacy of praying in the spirit (speaking in tongues) and its benefit to the human immune system, i.e., immunity enhanced by chemicals released from a part of the brain. I am attempting to clarify some information I have shared with a number of ministers. This is information that may

24. Taken from Simon Yap, "Medical Facts About Speaking in Tongues— Carl R. Peterson, M.D.," *His Grace Is Enough* (blog), June 14, 2011, https://hischarisisenough.wordpress.com/2011/06/14/medical-facts-about-speaking-in-tongues-carl-r-peterson-m-d/.

be deduced from what we know about the way the brain functions. We do know the part of the brain affected most noticeably by extended prayer [tongues] represents a significant portion of the brain and its metabolic activity. Therefore, voluntary speech during extended vocal prayer causes a major stimulation in these parts of the brain (mainly the hypothalamus).

The hypothalamus has direct regulation of four major systems of the body, mainly: a) the pituitary gland and all target endocrine glands; b) the total immune system; c) the entire autonomic system; and d) the production of brain hormones called endorphins and enkephalons, which are chemicals the body produces and are 100–200 times more powerful than morphine.

In summary, a very significant percentage of the central nervous system is directly and indirectly activated in the process of extended verbal and musical prayer [tongues] over a period of time. This results in a significant release of brain hormones which, in turn, increases the body's general immunity. It is further enhanced through the joyful laughter with increased respirations and oxygen intake to the brain, diaphragm and other muscles. This same phenomenon is seen in physical activity in general, i.e., running, etc.

...

Truly, we all benefit—body, soul, and spirit—from obedience and yielding to the Spirit of God in every area of our lives.[25]

---

25. Dr. Carl R. Peterson quoted in Simon Yap, "Medical Facts About Speaking in Tongues—Carl R. Peterson, M.D.," *His Grace Is Enough* (blog), June 14, 2011, https://hischarisisenough.wordpress.com/2011/06/14/medical-facts-about-speaking-in-tongues-carl-r-peterson-m-d/.

So, if you want to pray in tongues ten minutes a day, you'll get ten minutes of those secretions. That's not enough for me. That's why I pray hours a day in tongues, because I need those secretions. I didn't know it before, but I know it now. They boost our immune system by 35 to 40 percent!

Third John 2 (KJV) says, *"Beloved, I wish above all things that thou mayest prosper and be in health, even as thy soul prospereth."* If you want to jump-start the saving of your soul, then, I'm telling you, speak in tongues. That, in turn, is going to affect healing and health in your body.

10

READY, SET,
SAVE YOUR SOUL!

Let's review what we've learned about the saving of our souls:

1. It is the end, or goal, of our faith. (See 1 Peter 1:9.) The salvation of our souls is the outcome—the consummation—of our faith. It involves the salvation of our minds, our wills, our emotions, our thoughts, our feelings, and our affections.

2. There is a girding process that must take place. (See 1 Peter 1:13.) This is not God's job; He has nothing to do with it. We are the ones commanded to *"gird up the loins of our minds"* (KJV). Later, Peter instructs us to *"be holy"* (1 Peter 1:15), not to "get holy." But notice that this instruction comes *after* the command to gird up our mind. Unless we gird up the loins of our mind, we cannot be holy; and unless we are holy, we cannot see the Lord.

Also notice that it doesn't say to be holy when you feel like it or when the pastor is around or when you're with other Christians. It says to be holy *"in all manner of conversation"* (verse 15). Now God would not put that in the Bible if it could not be done. The original Greek word for *"gird up"* means to get your mind ready for action. The Greek word for *"loins"* (*osphus*) refers to the lower region of the back, the lumbar region, and, more specifically, the organs of reproduction. So when we're commanded to gird up the loins of our minds, we are to get the reproductive organs of our minds ready for action.

3. We must receive the engrafted Word. (See James 1:21.) Before you receive the engrafted Word, you must lay some things (any thought or idea that dirties the soul, any obscenity or that which causes shame) apart from your life. This is a daily process. If you do not lay these things aside, then your soul will not be saved. The Greek word for "lay aside" means to throw off, to cast away. In other words, chuck out that bad lumber; don't build with it!

What else are we to get rid of? The King James Version says, "All...superfluity of naughtiness." What does that mean? All abundance or excess of malice, ill will, and the desire to injure another person. You have to cast it all away, get rid of it before you can receive with meekness the Word of God. You have to make room for the Word in your life. Once you have thrown off all those things, the Word can take root in your heart! Remember: No root, no fruit! The Word itself has the ability, the resources, and the power to save your soul.

> All abundance or excess of malice, ill will, and the desire to injure another person. You have to cast it all away, get rid of it before you can receive with meekness the Word of God. You have to make room for the Word in your life. Once you have thrown off all those things, the Word can take root in your heart!

4. We must learn the power of focusing the mind on the Word. (See Joshua 1:8.) We are commanded to meditate on God's Word day and night, that it should not depart from our mouths. Why day and night? So we can *"observe to do according to all that is written therein"* (KJV). And then we will make our ways prosperous and have good success. Notice that it doesn't say that God will come down and live it for us. He already came down, then went back up, so we can do it for ourselves.

Colossians 3:1–2 tells us to focus our minds on things above. There's not a thing in there that says God will do it for us. The King James Version says, *"Set your affection on the things above"* (Colossians 3:2). The Greek word translated *"set your affection"* means "to exercise the mind"[26] and "[to] direct the mind to [a thing]."[27] In this Scripture, what are we commanded to direct our minds to? *"The things above,"* where Christ sits at the right hand of God.

5. We must construct, or frame, our minds with good lumber. (See Isaiah 26:3.) The word *"mind"* in this verse means to form a concept in the mind, to frame something, to use the imagination. God told me once, "Son, thoughts are like studs." So toss out every thought that comes to you that is not from God. Chuck it! Get rid of it. You need to frame with God's good lumber. Remember, we learned to test all lumber by the six criteria in Philippians 4:8: 1) It must be true, real, and credible; 2) it must be honorable, respectable, and venerable; 3) it has to be right, innocent, holy, just as it should be, evenhanded justice, and impartial; 4) it has to be pure, innocent, modest, chaste, and clean; 5) it must be

---

26. *phroneó, Strong's Exhaustive Concordance,* http://biblehub.com/greek/5426. htm.

27. *phroneó, Strong's Concordance,* http://biblehub.com/greek/5426.htm.

lovely, and that which causes pleasure or delight; 6) it must be of a good repute, a thought that deserves approval, is praiseworthy, and spoken in a kindly spirit.

6. We must give our souls verbal commands. (See Psalm 43:5.) If your soul is down, talk to it! Encourage it in the Lord! Also see Psalm 62:6–10, where David exhorts his soul to hope in God and not to be moved. We looked extensively at Psalm 103, which is a psalm of commands to the soul.

7. We can pray in tongues to promote health. (See Ephesians 4:23.) Now, you can only do this if you've been filled with the Holy Spirit! Remember, in the last chapter, that we looked at the research of Dr. Carl R. Peterson, who discovered that extended periods of speaking in tongues fortifies the human immune system, promoting health in the body. *The Amplified Bible* says, "*Be constantly renewed in the spirit of your minds [having a fresh mental and spiritual attitude]*" (Ephesians 4:23). The *Complete Jewish Bible* says it this way: "*And you must let your spirits and minds keep being renewed.*" I like that, because it reminds us that the condition of our spirit man is what enables us to bring our mind into alignment with the Word. If you take these seven points and put them into practice in your lives each and every day—and be diligent in doing them—your soul will be saved, changed, renewed, and in-line with the thoughts and purposes of God. And your life will be truly blessed!

* 9 7 8 1 7 3 4 5 2 7 3 4 6 *